W9-AKD-931

Por

Portuguese Water Dogs

and Other Working Dogs

Editorial:
Editor in Chief: Paul A. Kobasa
Project Manager: Cassie Mayer
Senior Editor: Christine Sullivan
Writer: Marta Segal Block
Researcher: Cheryl Graham
Manager, Contracts & Compliance
  (Rights & Permissions): Loranne K. Shields
Indexer: David Pofelski

Graphics and Design:
Manager: Tom Evans
Coordinator, Design Development
  and Production: Brenda B. Tropinski
Designer: Matthew Carrington
Cartographer: John Rejba

Pre-Press and Manufacturing:
Director: Carma Fazio
Manufacturing Manager:
  Steven K. Hueppchen
Production/Technology Manager:
  Anne Fritzinger

For information about other World Book publications, visit our Web site at http://www.worldbookonline.com or call 1-800-WORLDBK (967-5325).

For information about sales to schools and libraries, call 1-800-975-3250 (United States), or 1-800-837-5365 (Canada).

World Book, Inc.
233 N. Michigan Avenue
Chicago, IL 60601
U.S.A.

Library of Congress Cataloging-in-Publication Data
Portuguese water dogs and other working dogs.
    p. cm. -- (World Book's animals of the world)
    Includes index.
    Summary: "An introduction to Portuguese water dogs and other working dogs, presented in a highly illustrated, question-and-answer format. Features include fun facts, glossary, resource list, index, and scientific classification list"--Provided by publisher.
    ISBN 978-0-7166-1367-1
    1. Working dogs--Juvenile literature. 2. Portuguese water dog--Juvenile literature. I. World Book, Inc.
SF428.2.P67 2010
636.73--dc22
                                    2009020171

World Book's Animals of the World
Set 6: ISBN: 978-0-7166-1365-7
Printed in China by Leo Paper Products LTD., Heshan, Guangdong
1st printing November 2009

Picture Acknowledgments: Cover: © Jerry Shulman, SuperStock; © Lightcatch/Dreamstime; © Cynoclub/Dreamstime; © Rubberball/SuperStock; © Anna Sedneva, Shutterstock.

© Paul Bernhardt, Alamy Images 11; © Juniors Bildarchiv/Alamy Images 43; © Tristan Hawke, PhotoStockFile/Alamy Images 31; © Jeff Romeo, Alamy Images 25; © Tom Zuback, Alamy Images 55; AP Images 47; © Sonia Castleberry 23; © Dreamstime 17; © Cringuette/Dreamstime 4, 61; © Cynoclub/Dreamstime 3, 49; © Lightcatch/Dreamstime 9; © Manon Ringuette, Dreamstime 59; © pet-personalities.com/Hunter Portuguese Water Dogs 33; © Deborah Lee Miller, The Image Works 36; Melinda Harvey, Redwoods PWDs/Kokopelli Dog Training, Canton, CT 29; © Larry Downing, Reuters/Landov 7; © Johannes Eisele, Reuters/Landov 21; © Jonathan K. Li 53; © Jilian Rakow 59; © Nichol Talsma/Jenifer Hecker, Whiskers Pet Resort and Spa/Jilian Rakow 27; © Wendy Spradlin, Delta Society®/R.E.A.D® 39; © Helen Osler, Rex Features 15; © Shutterstock 5, 41, 45, 51; © Rubberball/SuperStock 19; © Jerry Shulman, SuperStock 37.

Illustrations: WORLD BOOK illustration by Roberta Polfus 13.

World Book's Animals of the World

Portuguese Water Dogs
and Other Working Dogs

WORLD BOOK

a Scott Fetzer company
Chicago
www.worldbookonline.com

Contents

What Is a Working Dog?

Many of the animals around us are pets. Pets, such as cats and dogs, offer people companionship. But in the past, cats and dogs were not just kept to keep people company. They had other important jobs to do. The term *working dog* describes dogs that were originally bred for such tasks as guarding houses, pulling sleds, and rescuing people. Working dogs are usually very smart and loyal.

The American Kennel Club (AKC), the group that records the purebred dogs in the United States, divides breeds of dogs into different groups. The working dogs are one group recognized by the AKC. Not all dogs that have jobs are in this group. For example, dogs that herd livestock on farms are in the AKC's herding group. And not all working dogs perform jobs for people.

Portuguese water dogs, or "Porties," are one breed of working dog. Until recently, they were not a well-known breed in the United States. But then in 2009, President Barack Obama and his family selected a Portuguese water dog as their family pet. Because of the Obamas' new dog, Bo, this dog breed suddenly became famous.

Bo, the Obama family dog

How Did Breeds of Working Dogs Develop?

A breed is a group of animals that have the same type of ancestors. Breeds of working dogs were developed for specific jobs. These dogs were bred all over the world, so they all have different histories.

Some working dogs still do the jobs for which they were bred. For example, some Saint Bernards (see page 48) still work in the mountains to rescue people. And, some Siberian *(sy BIHR ee uhn)* huskies still work as sled dogs. Other working dogs, however, such as Akitas *(ah KEE tahz),* have different jobs today. Akitas were originally bred in Japan to hunt deer and other animals. Today, many Akitas work as police dogs in Japan.

Most working dogs today serve as family pets.

Siberian huskies at work

When and Where Did the Portuguese Water Dog First Appear?

As their name suggests, Portuguese water dogs come from the European country Portugal. There, the dogs are called Cão d'Água *(kawn DAHG wah)*, which is Portuguese for "dog of water."

No one knows where the dogs came from before they arrived in Portugal. But experts believe the ancestors of the Portie were originally from central Asia and were brought to Europe by armies and traders. Once the dogs arrived in Portugal, they were kept and bred to help fishermen on their boats. With their strong swimming skills, the dogs were used for such jobs as retrieving nets. They also guarded the boat at shore.

By the early 1900's, larger boats had taken the place of small fishing boats, and Porties became less common. Then a breeding program in Portugal began in the 1930's to make sure the Portuguese water dog would not be lost as a breed.

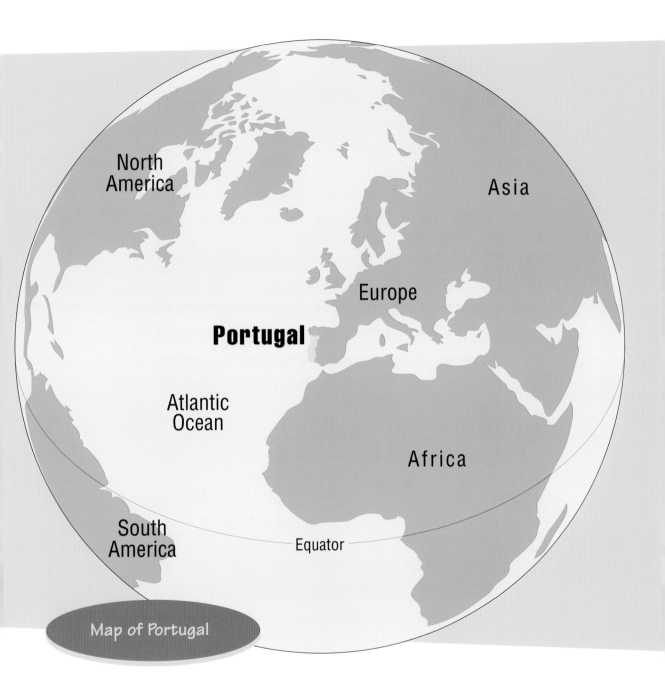

North
America

Asia

Europe

Portugal

Atlantic
Ocean

Africa

South
America

Equator

Map of Portugal

11

What Does a Portie Look Like?

Porties are medium-sized dogs. They stand around 20 inches (51 centimeters) tall at the shoulder and weigh between 35 and 60 pounds (16 and 27 kilograms). They are very muscular dogs.

Many dogs have two types of fur in their coats. They have short, soft fur, known as an undercoat, and a second coat of longer, coarser fur. The Portie, however, does not have an undercoat. Its outer coat is either curly or wavy, and it can come in many different combinations of colors, including black, brown, and white. Dark-colored Porties often have a patch of white fur on the chest.

Porties have another interesting trait. They have webbed feet. Skin in between their toes forms a webbing that helps them to swim better.

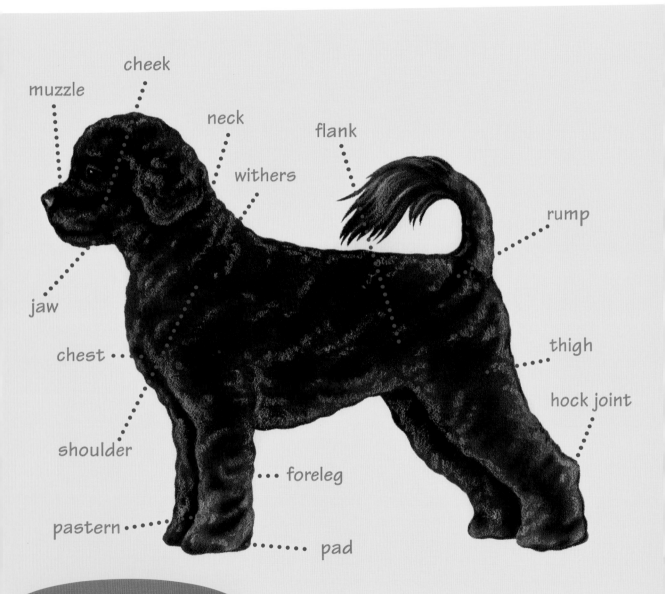

cheek

muzzle

neck

flank

withers

rump

jaw

chest

thigh

hock joint

shoulder

foreleg

pastern

pad

Diagram of a Portuguese
water dog

13

EAU CLAIRE DISTRICT LIBRARY

What Kind of Personality Might a Portie Have?

Porties love people. Many Portuguese water dogs pick one family member and form a special relationship with that person. These are social dogs, and they do not like to be left alone for long periods.

The Portie is described as being lively and very brave. Because Portuguese water dogs worked on boats retrieving things from the water, they tend to tug and chew on things, as many retrievers *(rih TREE vuhrz)* do. They are very smart and, if properly trained, they will follow even complicated commands that involve more than one step.

Porties have a lot of energy. They need much exercise and physical activity to be happy.

Porties can learn many tricks.

Is a Portie the Dog for You?

Owning a dog is a special job. Before you get a dog, you need to make sure you have enough time to take care of it. Porties need plenty of love and attention from their owners.

You also need to make sure that you have enough space. Portuguese water dogs need a lot of space for exercising. But, if you live near water, or love to go boating, then this may be a great dog for you.

Because they have no undercoat, Portuguese water dogs shed less and are considered to be a good choice for people with allergies. Before getting a dog, however, be sure to spend time with it so you will know if you're allergic to it. Some people with allergies are even allergic to Porties.

Porties need much exercise to stay happy.

17

What Should You Look for When Choosing a Portie Puppy?

Responsibility is a job or task you promise to do. A puppy is a big responsibility, but if you think you can handle it, you might begin to research different breeds by talking to a veterinarian or other dog owners. The Internet also has much information on specific breeds.

Once you have decided that a Portie is the right breed for you, you will need to find a good breeder. One way to find a breeder in the United States is to check with the club that specializes in your breed. The Portuguese Water Dog Club of America keeps a list of breeders for Porties. (See page 64 for a list of Web sites, including the site for this club.) Dog shows are another place where you might go to find dog breeders. And, you can see Porties in action at a dog show as they compete for championships.

Portie puppies

Should You Get an Older Portie Instead of a Puppy?

A puppy is not the right choice for every family. Puppies need a lot of training and attention. If your family does not have the time for that, an older dog might be a better choice. An older dog will usually be calmer and need less training.

There are many places to get an older Portie. Sometimes, a breeder has an older dog and decides the dog is not suitable for breeding. That does not mean the dog would not make a fine pet. Breeders will often sell older dogs in this situation.

Adopting an older dog from a previous owner can be a good idea. It can save a dog's life. But you need to be careful. If a grown Portie is not properly trained, he or she can be very difficult to control. Before adopting an adult dog, you need to make sure you know as much as possible about the dog's past, health, and personality.

The Portuguese Water Dog Club of America scouts around for Porties that have been abandoned or left in shelters and may be able to help you find an older dog. (See page 64 for this group's Web site address.)

An older Portie

What Does a Portie Eat?

Like people, dogs need a healthful diet with different nutrients (nourishing substances). However, dogs and people are different and should not eat the same food. Dogs should not be allowed to beg at the table or eat from people's plates. This can result in dogs eating too much food, or the wrong food.

In general, human food is not necessarily good for a dog, and some human foods can be dangerous. Chocolate contains a substance that is poisonous to dogs. Never give your dog chocolate. Other foods are bad for dogs too, including grapes and raisins, soft drinks, and sugarless candies.

Dog food is a better choice for your Portie. Ask your veterinarian to recommend the right type of dog food.

When you first bring your puppy home, you should keep feeding it the same food it is used to eating, on the same schedule. After the first few weeks, you can discuss changing the routine or food with your veterinarian.

A Portie waits patiently for its food.

Where Should a Portie Sleep?

When you first bring home a puppy, it may seem cozy to let your new pet sleep in your bed. However, it may be less cozy as the dog gets bigger. If you let a dog sleep in your bed as a puppy, it will be very hard to break it of the habit later on.

Dogs need their own space to feel comfortable. Many dog experts believe that a dog should have its own crate. A crate gives a dog a space to sleep and to feel safe. A dog crate is a big box with a large door. It may be made of metal wire or heavy plastic with many air holes. Make sure to get a crate large enough to comfortably hold the dog when it is fully grown.

You can also purchase a dog bed, or make a cozy sleeping area inside of your dog's crate by putting soft bedding inside. Remember, any bedding or toys you purchase to keep in the dog's bed must be washable. This will help protect your dog from fleas.

Many dogs like to rest in their own bed.

How Do You Groom a Portie?

Because Porties have no undercoat, they do not shed as much as other dogs. However, they still need brushing once or twice a week. And, every four to six weeks your dog will need to be fully groomed—that is, it will need to have a bath and get its nails and fur clipped. Since a Portie is so large, you will probably want to let a groomer bathe your dog and trim its nails and fur with special clippers.

Porties traditionally have their fur trimmed in one of two ways. The first, the "lion cut," was developed to make it easier for dogs to swim, while still keeping the dog's chest and belly warm. This cut has the fur on the hindquarters cut very short, but leaves the fur long elsewhere. With the second type of cut, the "retriever" cut, the dog has all its hair cut to a length of about one inch (2.54 centimeters). Dogs being shown in a dog show can have either a lion cut or a retriever cut.

A Portie at the groomer's

What About
Training a Portie?

Because of their large size and independent nature, it is very important that Porties be properly trained.

It is best to start reading about how to train your dog before you bring it home. You may also want to talk to people who own a Portuguese water dog and get advice on what types of problems may occur.

Training a dog will help it learn how to behave and how to communicate with you. If you get a puppy instead of an older dog, it is very important that you begin training it right away, before it can form bad habits.

There are books, videos, and Web sites on dog training. If you need more personal help, however, you can work one-on-one with a trainer, or you can take dog-training classes with other dog owners. Your veterinarian can probably help you find a local trainer in your area.

A Portie being trained

29

What Kinds of Exercise or Play Are Needed?

Porties need energetic exercise every day. Let your dog run freely outside in a fenced yard at least twice a day. Adult dogs should also be exercised by going on long walks, even if it is very cold or hot outside.

As you might have guessed, Porties love to go for a swim. This is another good way for your dog to get exercise. Just like people, dogs should not go swimming alone, and they should not go swimming in very cold or stormy weather.

Your Portie will also get exercise by playing with you. Make sure to have a variety of dog toys for your dog to enjoy.

Porties love to play.

Do Porties Like Water?

They do! These terrific swimmers were bred to work on fishing boats. The first written description of the Portie is a journal (diary) entry in 1297. The entry describes a Portuguese water dog saving a sailor's life. Today, these dogs will still jump into the water to retrieve things.

Your Portie must only be allowed to swim in a safe, clean body of water. Always follow this rule: Let adults decide when it's safe for your dog—or you—to go swimming.

Remember to towel dry your dog's fur after a swim or bath. Leaving its coat wet for too long could cause the dog to have skin problems.

A Portie playing fetch in the water

Should You Breed Your Portie?

Most people should not breed their dogs, however fun it sounds to have cute puppies around. There are many more pets in the world than people who want to take them in. It is estimated that up to 8 million dogs and cats go into shelters in the United States every year, and only about half of them find homes. One out of four dogs in shelters is a purebred.

The most helpful thing you can do is to have your vet perform an operation—called spay or neuter—on your dog that prevents it from being able to have puppies. This way, you do not make the problem of unwanted animals worse.

If you get a rescue dog, you may be asked to have your dog spayed or neutered. A good breeder may ask you to do the same.

Young Portie puppies

Are There Special Organizations for Portie Owners?

People who love dogs love to talk and share information about dogs. There are many local, national, and even international groups for dog owners. Because Porties are an unusual dog, their owners sometimes have a special attachment to the breed. There are many groups just for Portie owners.

There are national clubs for owners of Porties in Canada, the United Kingdom, and the United States. Dog organizations can be a good place to get recommendations on everything from breeders to obedience information.

You can find out more about these organizations by visiting the Web sites listed on page 64.

36

Happy Porties

37

How Do Porties Help People?

Some Portuguese water dogs still work on ships in Portugal. But because of their size, intelligence, and good nature, these dogs can be helpful in many other ways.

Porties are sometimes used as therapy dogs. Therapy dogs are dogs that have been trained to provide comfort to people in hospitals, nursing homes, or other stressful situations.

Porties and other working dogs can also be used to help teach children to read. There are groups that bring these dogs to schools to sit with children who have trouble reading. Sitting with a dog helps the student focus on reading.

Porties can also be trained to work as hearing dogs. These dogs help people who are deaf or hearing impaired. Hearing dogs listen for such noises as alarms. When such a noise sounds, the dog gets its owner's attention right away.

A Portie listens as its companion reads aloud.

What Are Some Other Working Dog Breeds?

The American Kennel Club (AKC) sets the standards (accepted rules) for dog breeds in the United States and keeps track of pedigrees. It divides dog breeds into groups. The AKC places the Portie into the working dog group. Other breeds in this AKC group include the boxer, Doberman pinscher *(DOH buhr muhn PIHN shuhr),* Great Dane, rottweiler *(ROT WY luhr),* Saint Bernard, and Siberian husky.

Groups similar to the AKC exist in Australia, Canada, and the United Kingdom. These organizations are the Australian National Kennel Council (ANKC); the Canadian Kennel Club (CKC); and the Kennel Club (KC), the United Kingdom's purebred organization. The Australian club groups breeds that the AKC considers to be working breeds differently. The Australians place the breeds of boxer, Doberman pinscher, Portuguese water dog, Saint Bernard, and Siberian husky in their utility group. In Australia, the Great Dane is placed in the nonsporting group.

A rottweiler

What Is a Komondor?

The komondor *(KOH mahn dawr)* is a large, white dog from Hungary. Experts think this dog was brought to Hungary from East Asia in the 1200's.

Ideally, a komondor is between 25 and 27 inches (63 and 69 centimeters) tall at the shoulder and weighs 100 pounds (45 kilograms) or more.

A full-grown komondor has both a soft undercoat and a heavy outer coat that falls to the ground in cords. These dogs were expected to live out in the open and guard livestock, such as flocks of sheep or goats. Some komondors still have this job today.

A komondor's unusual coat gives the dog protection from harsh weather. When komondors are puppies, their fur is soft and fluffy. As the dog ages, however, the cords form. If a dog's fur has not corded by the time it is 2 years old, it cannot compete in dog shows. The dog might be as old as 5 before its cords reach the ground. These dogs are bathed, but their fur is not combed or brushed once the cording begins.

A komondor

What Is a Boxer?

A boxer is a medium-sized dog that stands somewhere between 22 to 25 inches (56 to 64 centimeters) tall at the shoulder.

The ancestors of the boxer were bred for bull-baiting. Bull-baiting was a type of cruel sport in which dogs were encouraged to attack a bull. The practice was mostly stopped by the late 1800's. But all over Europe, there were dogs that had been bred for the sport. In Germany, that line of bull-baiting dogs was developed into the boxer. Today, boxers are often used as guard dogs.

Boxers are strong, energetic animals, so they need to be well trained. When trained, however, boxers are usually very reliable and protective of children, and they can make good family pets.

Boxers can be very happy in a city environment, even in an apartment, but they need much exercise.

A boxer

What Is a Great Dane?

Despite their name, Great Danes are not from Denmark. They are actually from Germany. Experts believe this breed came about around 400 years ago, when breeders crossed Irish wolfhounds and Old English mastiffs *(MAS tihfs).* No one knows why the breed name in English is "Great Dane." These dogs have many different names in other languages, almost all of which mean "large dog."

That name makes a lot of sense. Great Danes are one of the tallest dog breeds. Ideally, a Great Dane is at least 28 to 32 inches (71 to 81 centimeters) tall at the shoulder. Great Danes were originally bred for hunting boars (wild pigs). Boars are very dangerous, so it took a very large and brave dog to hunt them.

Although they are very large dogs, Great Danes are usually quite gentle. They are playful and patient with children, and they make good guard dogs. They need a lot of exercise and, of course, a lot of space.

A Great Dane

What Is a Saint Bernard?

The Saint Bernard is a large breed of dog with a comic and expressive face. Experts think the ancestors of this breed may have been brought to Europe from Asia by Roman soldiers. Saint Bernards were probably used for centuries in Europe for farm or herding work before they became rescue dogs.

In 1050, a monk named Bernard de Menthon founded a famous monastery in the Swiss Alps—tall mountains with snowy passes that are difficult to travel. Some pilgrims (religious travelers) used this route to travel to Rome. So Bernard turned the monastery into an inn to help these travelers on their difficult journey.

In the 1600's, someone brought in local dogs to help guard the inn. The monks living at the inn found that the dogs were good at finding paths that had been covered by snow. The dogs' keen sense of smell also helped them to find travelers who had been lost in an avalanche *(AV uh lanch)*—a wall of snow that suddenly slides down a mountainside. The dogs were so closely identified with the inn that people began to call them Saint Bernards. Saint Bernards are still used for this work today, even at the same inn.

A Saint Bernard

What Is a Siberian Husky?

The Siberian husky is a breed of sled dog. Siberia is a huge area of Russia. Some parts of Siberia are within the Arctic Circle. Ice and snow cover most of Siberia for about six months a year, so people use sleds to travel and to move goods over the snow and ice. A people native to Siberia, the Chukchi *(CHUK chee),* bred the Siberian husky to pull sleds.

As you can imagine, a dog bred for such a cold place must have a special coat. And, the Siberian does. It has a very thick, soft undercoat and a longer, coarser overcoat. The overcoat can be black, white, brown, or a mix of these colors. People who keep Siberian huskies as pets need to brush their dog's fur about once a week. They also need to be aware that the Siberian sheds heavily twice a year .

Dogs that pull a sled are very strong. Siberian huskies are only medium-sized dogs, but they are very powerful. Siberians can pull light loads for hours without getting tired. Sometimes, Siberians have been used to pull sleds of equipment on polar expeditions.

Though Siberian huskies are strong, they are known to have a friendly and gentle personality. They usually make fine family pets.

A Siberian husky

What Is a Dog Show Like?

Dog shows have become very popular in recent years. They are a way for owners to find out how well their dog conforms (matches up) to the standards (accepted rules) for its breed. In addition to being judged on looks, some dogs also compete in trials that judge how well they have been trained.

Dog shows are run by such organizations as the American Kennel Club (AKC) in the United States. The Canadian Kennel Club (CKC), the Kennel Club (KC) in the United Kingdom, and the Australian National Kennel Council (ANKC) also sponsor shows in their home countries. In addition, groups dedicated to individual breeds, such as the Portuguese Water Dog Club of America, sponsor shows for their breed. All of these groups have certain rules about how a dog must appear and behave. Many groups allow young people to participate in junior divisions at their shows.

Whether or not a dog is considered show quality has nothing to do with how good a dog it is, or what kind of pet it will make. Many dogs have traits that make them unacceptable in a show ring, but they make loving pets.

A Portie competes at a dog show.

Are There Dangers to Dogs Around the Home?

Dogs, even very large ones, are like babies in some ways. They like to explore things with their mouth. This means they often chew on or swallow things that can be dangerous. It is important to make sure all poisons are safely stored and that your dog cannot get to them.

Some plants are poisonous to dogs if eaten. If you have both houseplants and pets, ask your vet if the plants are safe to keep.

If you have any windows open, be sure they are not open wide enough for your dog to jump through. An excited dog may jump out the window before you have a chance to stop it.

Many pets are lost, injured, or killed each year because they were allowed to roam free. When a dog is outside, it must be on a leash with its person or inside a completely fenced area.

A Portie at home

What Are Some Common Signs of Illness?

Any change in your dog's behavior can be a sign of illness, so be sure to observe your dog closely every day. A dog that is ill or injured may be less active and may refuse to eat or may eat less. (Some illnesses, however, can cause a dog to eat or drink more.) Common signs of illness include a change in appetite, fever, vomiting, diarrhea, a dry nose, a dull coat, bald patches, unusual discharge from a dog's nose, ears, or eyes; and redness of the eyes.

Like many large dogs, Porties can suffer from hip problems as they get older. Older Porties may also suffer from cataracts, an eye problem.

Some Porties develop certain genetic diseases. Genes are the part of a cell that determines which characteristics (qualities) living things inherit from their parents. The number of Porties who are affected by genetic diseases is very small. But before buying a Portie, ask the breeder for proof that your dog's parents did not carry a genetic disease for which it can be tested.

Be sure to observe your dog every day for signs of illness.

What Routine Veterinary Care Is Needed?

Like people, dogs need regular medical checkups to stay healthy. Finding a good veterinarian is an essential first step to becoming a dog owner.

When you take your dog to the veterinarian, he or she will perform a physical exam, checking the dog for possible problems. Your dog will also need regular vaccinations *(VAK suh NAY shuhnz),* or shots. These shots help protect your dog from getting certain illnesses. Some dog illnesses, such as rabies, can be dangerous to people. Depending on where you live, the law may require you to make sure your dog has had vaccinations, and to keep a record of the shots.

Many vets recommend treating all puppies for parasitic worms until the puppies are three to four months old. Dogs in mosquito-infested areas should be given medicine the year around to prevent heartworms. A dog's annual checkup should include exams for heartworm and other worms.

A Portie puppy getting a checkup

What Are Your Responsibilities as an Owner?

You may already have certain responsibilities, such as taking care of a younger sibling, getting good grades, or keeping your room clean. Owning a dog gives you more responsibilities. If you choose to get a dog, you must honor those responsibilities, even if you are sick, tired, or just bored.

Some of the responsibilities of owning a dog include feeding, grooming, and caring for it. You must be sure to give your dog proper medical care, plenty of exercise, and a healthy diet. You also have a responsibility to clean up after your dog, and to make sure it does not harm or bother other people.

Owning a dog is a big responsibility, but the friendship you and your dog share may bring you much joy.

Owning a Portie or any dog
is a big responsibility.

Working Dog Fun Facts

→ Because the number of dogs used to develop the Portie breed was very small, doctors who study genes are very interested in Porties. In fact, Porties are one of the most studied dog breeds in the world.

→ The Giants are a baseball team in San Francisco. They use mostly Porties for their Baseball Aquatic Retrieval Korps (B.A.R.K.). These dogs retrieve homerun and batting practice balls that get hit into McCovey Cove, near the stadium. Money raised by selling the balls goes to charities.

→ The Newfoundland dog is one of the largest and strongest breeds of dog. Male Newfoundlands weigh about 140 pounds (64 kilograms) and stand about 28 inches (71 centimeters) tall at the shoulder! Females are slightly smaller.

→ Another working dog, the Akita, is from Japan. At one time, only members of the ruling family of Japan could own an Akita. Even today in Japan, small statues of Akitas are given as a sign of good luck on the birth of a child or during an illness.

Glossary

allergy A reaction, or change, caused by something that would not ordinarily be harmful to humans, such as animal fur or dust.

ancestor An animal from which another animal is directly descended. Usually, *ancestor* is used to refer to a relative more removed than a parent or grandparent.

breed To produce animals by carefully selecting and mating them for certain traits. Also, a group of animals having the same type of ancestors.

breeder A person who breeds animals.

groom To take care of an animal, for example, by combing, brushing, or trimming its coat.

livestock Farm animals; animals raised for their working ability or for their value as a source of food and other products.

neuter To operate on a male animal to make it unable to produce young.

parasite An organism (living creature) that feeds on and lives on or in the body of another organism, often causing harm to the being on which it feeds.

pedigree A record of an animal's ancestors.

purebred An animal whose parents are known to have both belonged to one breed.

rabies A disease caused by a virus that destroys part of the brain and almost always causes death. Rabies is transmitted by the bite of an animal that has the disease.

retriever A hunting dog trained to retrieve (find and bring back) game.

shed To throw off or lose hair, skin, fur, or other body covering.

spay To operate on a female animal to make it unable to have young.

trait A feature or characteristic particular to an animal or breed of animals.

Index (**Boldface** indicates a photo, map, or illustration.)

For more information about Portuguese water dogs and other working dogs, try these resources:

Books:
The Complete Dog Book for Kids by the American Kennel Club (Howell Book House, 1996)

Portuguese Water Dog (Comprehensive Owners Guide) by Paolo Correa (Kennel Club Books, 2005)

Working Dogs by Edward C. Haggerty (Grolier Educational, 1997)

Superpuppy: How to Choose, Raise, and Train the Best Possible Dog for You by Jill and Daniel Manus Pinkwater (Clarion Books, 2002)

Web sites:
American Kennel Club
http://www.akc.org

Australian National Kennel Council
http://www.ankc.org.au/

The Canadian Kennel Club
http://www.ckc.ca/en/

Humane Society of the United States
http://www.hsus.org

The Kennel Club (United Kingdom)
http://www.thekennelclub.org.uk/

Portuguese Water Dog Club of America
http://www.pwdca.org

The Portuguese Water Dog Club of Canada
http://www.pwdcc.org/

The Portuguese Water Dog Club of Great Britain
http://www.portuguesewaterdogs.org.uk/

Dog Classification

Scientists classify animals by placing them into groups. The animal kingdom is a group that contains all the world's animals. Phylum, class, order, and family are smaller groups. Each phylum contains many classes. A class contains orders, an order contains families, and a family contains genuses. One or more species belong to each genus. Each species has its own scientific name. Here is how the animals in this book fit into this system.

Animals with backbones and their relatives (Phylum Chordata)
Mammals (Class Mammalia)
Carnivores (Order Carnivora)
Dogs and their relatives (Family Canidae)

Domestic dog ....*Canis familiaris*